SCOTTISH COOKING
More Recipes from Scotland

by Sue McDougall

Sphere Books Ltd., 30-32 Gray's Inn Road, London WC1X 8JL

First published 1976
First published in this edition 1983
Reprinted 1984

© C.E.S.

*Use plain flour unless otherwise stated, castor sugar is
recommended for butter and sugar creamed mixtures.*

Printed and bound in Great Britain by BKT

FEATHER FOWLIE

A 3-4 lb. chicken	*3 eggs*	*2 teaspoons cream*
1 slice ham	*½ teaspoon thyme*	*2 pints water*
1 stick celery	*3 teaspoons chopped parsley*	*Salt and pepper*
1 small onion	*1 blade mace*	

Clean and joint the chicken. Soak in salted water for 30 minutes. Remove the chicken wash and then place in a large casserole. Cover with water and bring to the boil. Skim. Clean and cut up the celery. Skin and slice the onion. Add the celery, onion, ham, thyme, mace and parsley with salt and pepper to taste. Cover and simmer gently for 1½ hours. Remove the bird and ham. Skim any fat from the surface of the stock and then strain into another pan. Remove the meat from the chicken and mince with the ham. Add to the stock and heat gently for 15 minutes. Separate the yolks from the eggs and beat lightly. Remove the soup from the heat and add the strained egg yolks with the cream. Re-heat but do not boil.

POACHER'S SOUP

The Stock
3 lb. trimmings from venison or beef bones
3 pints water
1 stick celery
2 carrots

1 turnip
4 onions
2 teaspoons parsley
Salt and pepper

The Stock: Clean the bones and cover with water. Clean and cut up the celery. Peel and cut up the carrots and turnip. Skin and slice the onions. Add the vegetables, parsley and seasoning. Simmer for 3 hours. Strain into another pan.

The Soup
1 woodstock or pheasant
or brace partridges
or grouse
or a rabbit or a hare

1 oz. seasoned flour
½ oz. fat
1 onion
½ lb. potatoes
3 sticks celery

1 small white cabbage
Pinch black pepper
Pinch allspice
Salt and pepper

The Soup: Skin and clean the meat. Cut into joints and dip into seasoned flour. Melt the fat in a frying pan. Skin and slice the onion and fry until it begins to brown. Fry the pieces of meat until they begin to brown. Add, with the onions to the stock. Clean and cut up the celery. Peel and cut up the potatoes. Clean and quarter the cabbage and add with the potatoes to the soup. Season and simmer until the meat is cooked.

GROUSE SOUP

The Stock
Marrowbone
3 rashers streaky bacon
2 sticks celery
3 pints water

6 black peppercorns
Pinch cayenne pepper
Salt and pepper

The Stock: Clean the bone. Put in a pan and cover with water. Cut up the bacon and add to the water. Clean and break up the celery and add to the pan. Season and bring to the boil. Skim well. Simmer for 2 hours then strain into a large saucepan or casserole.

Pair grouse
1 oz. bacon fat
½ oz. seasoned butter
Butter for frying
2 oz. coarse oatmeal

Salt and pepper
1 tablespoon cream or
1 tablespoon red wine and
1 teaspoon whisky

The Soup: Clean and pluck the birds. Coat the breasts with bacon fat and put a nub of seasoned butter inside each. Cook for 30 minutes in a moderately hot oven (375°F. 191°C. gas mark 5). Remove all the meat from the birds and mince — except the breasts. Melt the butter in a pan and fry the oatmeal until lightly brown. Stir in the stock and add the minced meat, Simmer for 20 minutes. Dice the breasts and lightly fry in butter. Add to the soup. Remove from the heat and add the cream or wine.

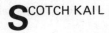COTCH KAIL

1½ lb. mutton
2 onions
1 leek
1 white cabbage

½ oz. pearl barley
3 pints water
Salt and pepper

Clean the meat and remove any excess fat. Place the meat in a large pan or casserole. Cover with water. Skin and dice the onions. Discard the outer green leaves of the leak and cut it into small pieces. Add the onions, leek and barley to the pan. Bring to the boil and simmer for 2 hours until the meat is cooked. Skim off any fat from the surface. After the soup has been cooking for 1 hour, cut up the heart of the cabbage and add to the soup. When cooked, remove the meat and cut into pieces. Place in a tureen and pour the soup over the meat.

HOTCH POTCH — HAIRST BREE

2 lb. neck of lamb
1 carrot
½ turnip
1 small cauliflower
1 lettuce

2 oz. shelled green peas
2 oz. broad beans
1 onion
1 tablespoon chopped parsley
Salt and pepper

Cut the meat into pieces and remove as much fat as possible. Put in a large saucepan and cover with cold water with 1 teaspoon salt. Bring to the boil and skim. Simmer gently for 1 hour. Peel the turnip and carrot and dice. Skin and cut up the onion. Add the turnip, carrot, onion, beans and half the peas to the stock. Season. Simmer for a further 1½ hours. Wash and shred the lettuce. Wash the cauliflower and break into small sprigs. Add the lettuce and cauliflower with the rest of the peas to the soup. Simmer for 30 minutes. Add the parsley before serving.

POWSODI – SHEEP'S HEAD BROTH

Sheep's head and trotters	2 leeks	5 pints water
2 carrots	4 oz. shelled peas	2 teaspoons chopped parsley
1 small turnip	2 onions	Salt and pepper
1 stick celery	2 oz. pearl barley	

Wash and soak the head and trotters in water overnight. Remove the glassy parts of the eyes, scrape the head and trotters and scrub clean. Split the head and remove the brains and put them in a little vinegar. Put the head, barley and 1 teaspoon of salt and a pinch of pepper in a large saucepan of water. Bring to the boil, skim and simmer for 2½ hours or longer if the sheep was an old one. Skim. Peel and dice the carrots and turnip. Discard the coarser outer green leaves of the leeks and chop them up into small pieces. Skin and dice the onions. Cut up the celery. Add the vegetables to the stock. Simmer for a further hour. Remove the head and trotters and add the chopped parsley to the broth. Slice some of the meat from the head and return to the broth. The rest of the meat and tongue may be served with brain sauce.

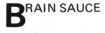RAIN SAUCE

1 oz. flour
½ pint broth from sheep's head

½ pint milk
Sheep's brain

Remove the brains from the vinegar, wash, then simmer in salted water. Drain and cut up. Work the flour into a little of the sheep's broth. Stir in the rest of the broth and the milk. Simmer gently for 2-3 minutes. Cut the rest of the meat from the sheep's head (see opposite) and the tongue into slices. Pour the sauce over the meat.

HIGHLAND HOTPOT

1 brace grouse
1 small rabbit
3 rashers streaky bacon
2 sticks celery
2 medium-sized onions

4 potatoes
½ small white cabbage
1 tablespoon red wine
Salt and pepper

Clean the grouse and rabbit and cut into joints. Cut up the bacon. Clean and cut up the celery. Skin and dice the onions. Peel and slice the potatoes. Place the meat and vegetables in layers in an ovenproof casserole. Season. Half fill the dish with water and bring to the boil. Wash and shred the cabbage and add with the wine to the casserole. Cover and cook in a moderate oven (350°F. 177°C. gas mark 4) for 2½ hours.

TWEED KETTLE

2 lb. fresh salmon
1 shallot or
1 tablespoon chopped chives
1 tablespoon chopped parsley

½ pint water
½ pint white wine
Pinch ground mace
Salt and pepper

Clean the fish and place in a fish kettle or large pan. Cover with water and simmer gently for 5 minutes. Remove the fish and keep the fish stock. Skin and cut up the salmon into 1 inch cubes free from bones. Skin and cut up the shallot. Replace the fish in the kettle with ½ pint of the fish stock, the wine and shallot or chives. Season. Cover and simmer for 25 minutes. Add the chopped parsley before serving.

TROUT FRIED IN OATMEAL

Trout
½ oz. coarse oatmeal per fish
¼ oz. butter per fish
Salt and pepper
Parsley
Lemon wedges

Clean the trout. Cut open and remove the backbone. Melt the fat in a frying pan. Season the oatmeal and roll the fish in it. Fry the fish in the butter until golden brown on both sides. Drain on kitchen paper. Serve garnished with parsley and lemon wedges.

HAM AND HADDIE

1 smoked Moray Firth haddock
2 slices smoked ham
1 oz. butter
Pepper

Place the haddock in a pan and cover with water.
Simmer for 2 minutes. Turn the fish and simmer
for a further 2 minutes. Take out the fish and
remove the skin and bones. Melt the butter in a
frying pan and place the ham slices on it. Turn
once and place the fish on top. Season with pepper.
Cover and simmer for 2-3 minutes.

TATTIES AN 'HERRIN'

Herrings
Potatoes
Salt

Peel the potatoes or scrub them well and place in a large saucepan. Cover with water. Season and bring to the boil. Wash and clean the herrings. When the potatoes are half cooked, pour away most of the water. Place the herrings over the potatoes. Put the lid on the saucepan and heat very gently so that the potatoes and fish cook in the steam from the remaining water.

POTTED SALMON

8 oz. cold cooked salmon
1 tablespoon anchovy paste
4 oz. butter
Pinch mace
Pinch cayenne
Salt and pepper

Finely mash the salmon which should be free from bones. Mix with the anchovy paste. Add the seasoning and butter until the mixture is smooth and of the required consistency. Pot in cold, sterilized jars and cover with melted butter.

CREAMED FINNAN-HADDIE

1 smoked haddock
1 oz. grated cheese
1 oz. butter
½ pint white sauce

Clean the fish and place in a pan with just enough
water to cover it. Simmer gently for 2 minutes on
each side. Take out the fish. Remove the skin and
bones and cut the fish into small pieces. Place in
an ovenproof dish.

The Sauce
½ pint milk
¾ oz. butter
¾ oz. flour

1 oz. grated cheese
Pinch mustard
Salt and pepper

The Sauce: Melt the butter in a saucepan and work in the flour using a wooden spoon. Warm until the mixture bubbles. Remove from the heat and stir in the milk. Return to the heat and warm for 2-3 minutes, stirring continuously. Add the cheese and mustard. Season. Stir until the cheese dissolves in the sauce but do not re-heat. Pour the sauce over the haddock, sprinkle with cheese and dot with butter. Place under the grill and brown.

COLLOPS IN THE PAN

4 slices rump or fillet steak
½ oz. butter
2 onions

2 teaspoons oyster pickle or walnut pickle
Salt and pepper

Skin and slice the onions. Melt the butter in a frying pan and add the onions. Heat until the onions are softened but not coloured. Push them to one side and put the steak in the pan. Brown and seal quickly on both sides. Arrange the onions around the meat. Season. Cover and cook quickly for 10 minutes. When cooked, place the steaks on a warm platter. Stir the oyster pickle or walnut pickle into the pan. Bring to the boil, heat for 1 minute and pour over the steaks. Serve with jacket potatoes and green vegetables.

MINCE CHICKEN

4 oz. white cooked chicken meat
2 oz. mushrooms
2 oz. butter
2 oz. flour
¾ pint stock

Salt and pepper
½ teaspoon chopped parsley
½ teaspoon chopped chives
2 tablespoons cream
Few drops lemon juice

Peel and mince the mushrooms. Heat gently in a little of the butter in a covered pan for 15 minutes. Melt the remaining butter in another pan and work in the flour using a wooden spoon. Stir in the stock, bring to the boil and simmer until smooth. Mince the cooked chicken and add with the mushrooms to the stock. Add the parsley, chives and a few drops of lemon juice. Heat gently for a few minutes and season to taste. Remove from the heat and stir in the cream. Serve with creamed potatoes or rice and buttered peas.

GALANTINE OF VENISON AND PORK

3 lb. thick breast venison
1 lb. minced pork or sausage-meat
½ lb. ham
3 eggs
3 cloves garlic

Sprig thyme and marjoram
6 black peppercorns
4 pints water
Salt and pepper

Bone the venison and remove any gristle. Boil the
venison bones with the water, seasoned with the
herbs and salt. Cut the ham into small pieces and
mix with the minced pork and garlic. Boil the eggs
hard and cut in half. Lay the boned venison on a
board. Cover with half the minced pork mixture,
then add the eggs and then the rest of the pork.
Season. Roll up the venison and put in a floured
cloth. Remove the bones from the stock. Place the
venison in its cloth in the stock, cover and simmer
for 4 hours. Top up with water if necessary. Leave

to cool in the water. When cold, remove from the stock and place in a dish that just fits it. Cover with foil and put a weight on top. Leave in the refrigerator overnight. Serve cold, sliced, with green salad.

KINGDOM OF FIFE PIE

1 rabbit
½ lb. pickled pork
1 egg
½ pint beef stock

Forcemeat balls
Rough puff pastry
Salt and pepper

Skin and clean the rabbit, keeping the liver aside. Divide into joints. Dice the pork. Hard boil the egg and slice. Place the rabbit, pork, egg with the forcemeat balls in a pie dish and add the stock. Season. Cover with rough puff pastry. Cook in a hot oven (450°F. 232°C. gas mark 8) for 30 minutes until the pastry is risen and golden brown and then in a warm oven (325°F. 163°C. gas mark 3) for 40 minutes until the meat is tender when tested with a skewer.

Forcemeat
1 rabbit liver
1 rasher bacon
4 oz. breadcrumbs
1 tablespoon parsley
1 tablespoon thyme
Salt and butter
Milk

Forcemeat balls: Simmer the liver in salted water for 10 minutes. Mince the liver and chop up the bacon. Mix all the ingredients together and bind with a little milk.

MUTTON PIES

Hotwater Pastry
1 lb. flour
4 oz. beef dripping
½ pint water
½ teaspoon salt

The Pastry: Gently heat the dripping with the water until it boils. Put the flour into a basin and make a hole in the centre. Pour the dripping/water mixture into the flour and work in quickly with a knife. When cool enough to handle form into a lump and turn out onto a floured board. Knead lightly. Roll-out and cut out six circles using a tumbler. Line six pattie tins. Fill each tin with the meat mixture.

Filling
12 oz. lean mutton
1 small minced onion or shallot
½ teaspoon ground mace or nutmeg
4 tablespoons beef stock or water

Salt and pepper
1 teaspoon Worcestershire sauce or
* mushroom ketchup*

The Filling: Remove any skin or bone from the meat. Cut the meat into small pieces. Mix all the ingredients together, moistened with the beef stock. Cut six lids from the remaining pastry. Moisten the edges of the pastry cases and close with the lids. Brush with beaten egg or milk. Make a hole in each. Cook for 15 minutes in a hot oven (425°F. 218°C gas mark 7) for 15 minutes until the paste is brown. Cook for a further 20 minutes in a moderate oven (350°F. 177°C. gas mark 4) until the meat is cooked.

CHICKEN STOVIES

A 3-4 lb. chicken
2 lb. potatoes
1 onion
1 oz. butter
Salt and pepper

Clean and dry the chicken. Cut into pieces. Peel the potatoes and slice thickly. Skin and slice the onion. Place alternate layers of potato, chicken and onion in a casserole. Season each layer with salt and pepper and dot the potatoes with butter. Just cover the mixture with water. Close the dish and cook in a moderate oven (350°F. 177°C. gas mark 4) for 1 hour until the meat is cooked.

CHEESE POTATO CAKES

½ lb. hot, boiled, mashed potatoes
½ oz. butter
2 oz. flour
4 oz. grated cheese
2 eggs
2 oz. breadcrumbs
Fat for frying

Add the butter and a pinch of salt to the potatoes. Work the flour into the potatoes and add the cheese. Beat the eggs and add to the mixture. Shape into round cakes, dip into breadcrumbs and fry in hot fat.

ARRAN POTATO SALAD

3 lb. potatoes
4 oz. shelled or frozen peas
2 oz. beetroot
1 teaspoon chopped tarragon

1 teaspoon chopped chervil
1 teaspoon chopped parsley
1 teaspoon chopped shallot
Salt and pepper

Peel and boil the potatoes in salted water. Cook the peas and beetroot. Dice the vegetables and mix with the herbs and shallot. Toss in the salad dressing.

Salad Dressing
3 tablespoons olive oil
1 tablespoon wine vinegar

Salad Dressing: Mix the olive oil and vinegar together.

OATMEAL BISCUITS

4 oz. flour
2 oz. medium oatmeal
2 oz. fine oatmeal
2 teaspoons baking powder
1 oz. butter

1 oz. cooking fat
2 oz. castor sugar
1 egg
2 tablespoons milk
Pinch salt

Mix the flour, oatmeal, salt and baking powder together. Rub in the fats and stir in the sugar. Lightly beat the egg and add with the milk to the flour mixture. Knead lightly and roll out to a ¼ inch thickness. Cut into rounds and place on a lightly greased tray. Prick all over and bake for 15-20 minutes in a moderate oven (350°F. 177°C. gas mark 4).

PITCAITHLY BANNOCK

8 oz. flour
4 oz. butter
3 oz. castor sugar

1 oz. blanched almonds
1 oz. orange or citron peel

Blanch and skin the almonds and finely chop the orange peel. Mix the nuts and peel together. Knead the butter and sugar together by hand. Work the flour and peel and nuts into the butter/sugar mixture by hand. Knead lightly until smooth. Press with the hand into a round about ½ – ¾ inch thick. Place in a lightly greased sheet of greaseproof paper on a baking sheet. Place the bannock on the baking sheet and cook in a warm oven (325°F. 163°C. gas mark 3) for 50 minutes. Sprinkle with castor sugar and cool on a wire tray.

FIFE BANNOCKS

6 oz. flour
4 oz. oatmeal
½ teaspoon bicarbonate of soda
¾ teaspoon cream of tartar
½ teaspoon sugar

¼ oz. lard
4 tablespoons buttermilk or
  thick sour milk
Pinch salt

Mix all the dry ingredients together and rub in the lard. Add milk to make a soft-dough. Turn on to a floured board and knead lightly. Roll into a round. Cut in four and bake on a hot girdle or a thick-bottomed frying pan.

BUTTERY ROWIES

1 lb. flour	6 oz. butter
1 oz. baker's yeast or	6 oz. lard
2 teaspoons dried yeast	¾ pint tepid water
½ oz. castor sugar	Small teaspoon salt

Sift the flour and salt into a warm bowl. Cream the yeast with the castor sugar. Add to the flour with the water. Mix well. Cover with a damp towel and stand in a warm place to rise for 30 minutes, or until its volume has doubled. Blend the butter and lard together and divide into three. Roll out the dough into a long strip. Cut one portion of the fat mixture into tiny pieces and dot evenly over the top two thirds of the strip of dough. Fold the fatless dough over the centre third and the top third down, like an envelope, as for flaky pastry.

Press the sides together and turn the pastry half-way round. Roll out into a long strip again. Repeat with the second and then the third portion of fat, letting the dough rest for 30 minutes between each addition of fat. Roll out and cut into small rounds or ovals. Place, well apart, on a floured baking sheet. Cover and leave to stand in a warm place for 45 minutes. Bake in a moderately hot oven (400°F. 204°C. gas mark 6).

BAPS

½ lb. flour
1 teaspoon salt
½ teaspoon sugar
1 oz. cooking fat

½ oz. yeast
4 tablespoons milk
4 tablespoons water

Sieve the flour and salt into a warm bowl and rub in the fat. Make a well in the middle of the mixture. Cream the yeast and sugar together and add to the warm milk and water. Make a well in the middle of the flour and pour the yeast mixture into this. Mix well. Knead lightly until smooth. Dust with flour, cover with a cloth and leave in a warm place to rise for 1 hour or until the dough has doubled in size. Divide into six flat ovals. Place, well apart, on a greased baking tray. Cover and leave for 15 minutes. Brush with milk and bake in a hot oven (400°F. 204°C. gas mark 6) for 15-20 minutes.

PETTICOAT TAILS

12 oz. flour
6 oz. butter
1½ oz. castor sugar

½ gill milk
2 teaspoons caraway seeds (optional)

Mix the caraway seeds, if used, with the flour.
Melt the butter in the milk. Make a hole in the
middle of the flour and pour the butter/milk into
it. Knead lightly until the mixture comes together.
Turn on to a lightly floured board and roll out to a
¼ inch thickness. Lay an inverted dinner plate on
the paste and cut out a large circle. Remove the
plate. Place a tumbler in the centre of the circle of
paste and cut out a small circle. Keep the smaller
circle whole but cut the outer part into segments
or tails. Do not cut right through the paste. Bake
on a greased baking tray in a moderate oven
(350°F. 177°C. gas mark 4) for 20 minutes until
crisp and golden. Cool on a wire rack and dust
with castor sugar.

SCOTS CRUMPETS

4 oz. flour
1 oz. sugar
1 teaspoon bicarbonate of soda
2 teaspoons cream of tartar

1 teaspoon melted butter
1 egg
¼ pint milk
Oil for frying

Sift the flour, bicarbonate of soda and cream of tartar together. Mix in the sugar. Lightly beat the egg and then stir, with the melted butter, into the flour mixture. Add enough milk to give the consistency of thick cream. If possible, leave to stand about an hour. Brush a hot girdle or thick frying pan with oil. Drop several spoonfuls of the batter on to the pan. Tilt the pan to spread the batter thinly. After 2 minutes, when cooked on one side, turn and cook the other side. Drain on kitchen paper and place between warm tea towels to keep the crumpets moist. Serve buttered.

SAUCER PANCAKES

2 oz. flour
2 oz. butter
2 oz. castor sugar

2 eggs
½ pint milk
Jam

Grease 12 small patty tins or 6 saucers. Cream the butter and sugar. Beat the eggs into the mixture, one at a time, adding a little flour if necessary to prevent curdling. Fold in the rest of the flour. Slightly warm the milk and add to the mixture. (Curdling at this stage does not matter.) Half fill the patty tins or saucers and bake in a fairly hot oven (375°F. 191°C. gas mark 5) for 10-15 minutes. Turn out on to kitchen paper and dust with sugar. If patty tins are used, sandwich the pancakes together with jam. If saucers are used, cover half of each pancake with jam and fold over.

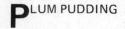LUM PUDDING

6 oz. flour
6 oz. breadcrumbs
6 oz. suet
6 oz. sugar
6 oz. raisins
6 oz. currants
3 oz. chopped mixed peel

1 teaspoon baking powder
½ teaspoon salt
½ teaspoon ground mace
½ teaspoon grated nutmeg
2 eggs
1 tablespoon brandy
½ pint milk

Wash, dry and stone the fruit. Finely shred the suet. Mix all the dry ingredients together. Lightly beat the eggs. Add the eggs and brandy with enough milk to bind the mixture together. Turn into a well greased basin and steam for 6-7 hours. Serve with brandy sauce.

The Sauce
1 tablespoon brandy
1 tablespoon Madeira
⅓ pint water
1 oz. butter
½ oz. castor sugar

The Sauce: Put the butter in a basin that is standing in a bowl of hot water until the butter melts. Stir in the sugar, brandy and Madeira. Pour over the pudding or serve separately.

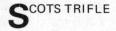SCOTS TRIFLE

6 sponge cakes
18 ratafia biscuits
Raspberry jam
Grated rind ½ lemon
1 gill sherry

1 tablespoon brandy
¾ pint custard
½ pint cream
Castor sugar
Drambuie

Cut the sponge cakes in half and spread with jam. Arrange in a glass dish. Pound the ratafias and spread over the sponges. Sprinkle with the grated lemon rind. Over this, pour the sherry and the brandy. Add the custard and allow to stand for 1 hour. Whip the cream and flavour with sugar and Drambuie. Pile over the custard.

DIET LOAF

1 lb. sugar	Grated peel 1 lemon
6 eggs	½ teaspoon ground cinnamon
12 oz. flour	Icing sugar
8 oz. butter	

Cream the butter and sugar. Beat the eggs and add to the butter/sugar mixture. Beat well together (20 minutes by hand). Add the grated lemon rind and cinnamon. Gradually stir in the flour, beating well after each addition. Line a baking tin with well greased greaseproof paper and pour in the sponge. Bake in a moderate oven (375°F. 191°C. gas mark 5) for 35 minutes, until the sponge is a pale golden brown. Ice when cold.

CALEDONIAN CREAM

1 tablespoon Dundee orange marmalade
1 tablespoon sugar
1 tablespoon brandy or Highland unblended
 malt whisky
½ lemon
1 pint cream

Add the marmalade, sugar, brandy or whisky and
the juice of half a lemon to the cream. Whisk well.
Turn into a mould and chill.

ROWAN JELLY

3 lb. rowan berries
1 lb. cooking apples
Granulated or loaf sugar

Wash the berries and remove the stalks. Drain. Wash the apples and cut them up, discarding the cores. Place the fruit in a preserving pan and add enough water to just cover the fruit. Simmer gently for 45 minutes. Strain through a jelly cloth. Measure the liquid as it is returned to the pan and allow 1 lb. sugar for each pint of liquid. Stir until the mixture boils and all the sugar has dissolved. Continue heating until setting point is reached — about half an hour — when a drop of the liquid sets quickly on a cold plate. Skim and pour into sterilized jars and seal.

ORKNEY CHEESE

8 pints milk
1 teaspoon rennet
½ teaspoon salt

Heat the milk to 85°F. 29°C. Add the rennet and a little water. Stir with a wooden spoon for 5 minutes. Leave to stand for 30 minutes to form a smooth curd. Cut the curd in several directions using a bread knife. Let it stand for 15 minutes. Stir and strain through a cheese cloth. Break up the curd with the hand and mix in the salt. Place in a cheese cog or chessit with the cloth underneath. Cover the top with the cloth, replace the lid and put a 7 lb. weight on it. Leave for 8 days, changing the cloth each day and increasing the weights if necessary. When dry, store in oatmeal.

ATHOLL BROSE

3 oz. oatmeal
2 tablespoons liquid heather honey
1 pint water
Whisky

Add the water to the oatmeal until a thick paste is formed. Leave to stand for ½ hour and then pass through a fine strainer, pressing the mixture against the strainer with a wooden spoon. Discard the meal. Mix the creamy liquid with the honey. Stir and make up to 2 pints with whisky. Serve alone or topped with whipped cream sprinkled with fine lightly toasted oatmeal.

Index

Arran potato salad, 30

Atholl brose, 47

Baps, 36

Brain sauce, 11

Buttery rowies, 34

Caledonian cream, 44

Cheese potato cakes, 29

Chicken stovies, 28

Collops in the pan, 20

Creamed finnan-haddie, 18

Diet loaf, 43

Feather fowlie, 3

Fife bannocks, 33

Galantine of venison and pork, 22

Grouse soup, 6

Hairst bree, 9

Ham and haddie, 15

Highland hotpot, 12

Kingdom of Fife pie, 24

Mince chicken, 21

Mutton pies, 26

Oatmeal biscuits, 31

Orkney cheese, 46

Petticoat tails, 37

Pitcaithly bannock, 32

Plum pudding, 40

Poacher's soup, 4

Potted salmon, 17

Powsodie, 10

Rowanjelly, 45

Saucer pancakes, 39

Scotch kail, 8

Scots crumpets, 38

Scots trifle, 42

Tatties an herrin, 16

Trout fried in oatmeal, 14

Tweed kettle, 13